Pebble®
Plus

GREAT ASIAN AMERICANS

Michelle Kwan

by Stephanie Cham

CAPSTONE PRESS
a capstone imprint

Pebble Plus is published by Capstone Press,
1710 Roe Crest Drive, North Mankato, Minnesota 56003
www.mycapstone.com

Library of Congress Cataloging-in-Publication Data
Names: Cham, Stephanie, author.
Title: Michelle Kwan / by Stephanie Cham.
Description: North Mankato, Minnesota : Capstone Press, 2018. | Series:
    Pebble plus. Great Asian Americans.
Identifiers: LCCN 2017044056 (print) | LCCN 2017044882 (ebook) |
ISBN 9781515799795 (eBook PDF) | ISBN 9781515799580 (hardcover) |
ISBN 9781515799733 (pbk.)
Subjects: LCSH: Kwan, Michelle, 1980---Juvenile literature. | Figure
    skaters—United States—Biography—Juvenile literature. | Women figure
    skaters—United States—Biography--Juvenile literature. | Asian
    Americans—Biography—Juvenile literature. | Asian American
    women--Biography—Juvenile literature.
Classification: LCC GV850.K93 (ebook) | LCC GV850.K93 C53 2018 (print) | DDC
    796.91/2092 [B] –dc23
LC record available at https://lccn.loc.gov/2017044056

Editorial Credits
Abby Colich, editor; Juliette Peters, designer;
Morgan Walters, media researcher; Kathy McColley, production specialist

Photo Credits
Alamy: PCN Photography, 7, 9, ZUMA Press Inc, 21; ASSOCIATED PRESS: JON FREILICH,
11; Getty Images: The Asahi Shimbun, 13, Theo Wargo, Cover; Newscom: BRIAN SNYDER/
REUTERS, 19, GRIGORY DUKOR/REUTERS, 17, JERRY LAMPEN/REUTERS, 15, Kyodo
News, 5; Shutterstock: Attitude, design element throughout, j avarman, (pattern) design element
throughout, most popular, design element throughout

Note to Parents and Teachers

The Great Asian Americans set supports standards related to biographies. This
book describes and illustrates the life of Michelle Kwan. The images support
early readers in understanding the text. The repetition of words and phrases
helps early readers learn new words. This book also introduces early readers
to subject-specific vocabulary words, which are defined in the Glossary
section. Early readers may need assistance to read some words and to use
the Table of Contents, Glossary, Read More, Internet Sites, Critical Thinking
Questions, and Index sections of the book.

Printed and bound in the USA.
010771S18

Table of Contents

Childhood on Ice

Michelle Kwan was born in 1980.

Her parents were from Hong Kong.

Her brother played hockey.

Her sister was a figure skater.

Michelle wanted to skate too.

1980
born July 7 in
Torrance, California

Michelle started lessons
at age 5. She skated
every day. Soon she joined
her first contest. She came
in first.

1986
wins her first
skating contest

1980

In 1992 Michelle wanted to skate at the senior level. Her coach wanted her to train as a junior. Michelle took the senior test anyway. She passed. Her coach made her work harder.

1992
passes senior level
skating test

1980   1986

In 1994 Michelle skated

in a world contest. She won!

She tried out for the Olympics.

She did not make the team.

She was the backup.

1994
wins the World Junior
Championships
tries out for
the Olympics

1980   1986   1992

Michelle at the 1994 U.S.
Figure Skating Championships

Skating on Top of the World

In 1996 Michelle skated
for the U.S. and world titles.
She won both! In 1998 she went
to the Olympics. She wanted
a gold medal. She got a silver.

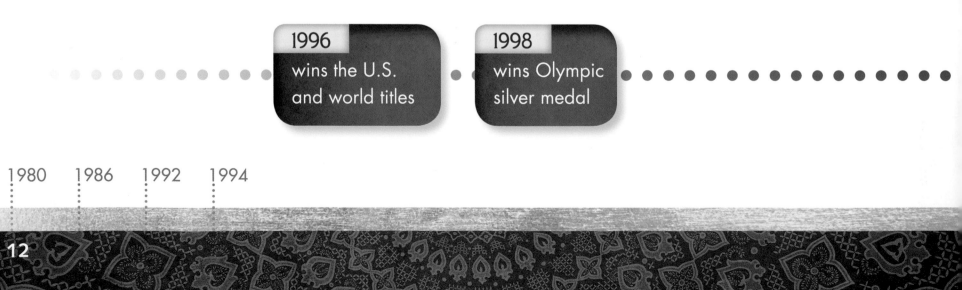

1996
wins the U.S. and world titles

1998
wins Olympic silver medal

1980   1986   1992   1994

Michelle at the
1998 Olympics

Michelle kept winning. She won
nine U.S. titles. She won
five world titles. She went
to the Olympics again in 2002.
She won a bronze medal.

2002
wins Olympic
bronze medal

2002 Olympic figure skating winners

15

Michelle tried for the world
title again in 2005. It was
her last contest. She hurt
her hip and leg. She couldn't
go to the Olympics.

2005
comes in
fourth at World
Championships

2006
drops out of
Olympics

1980   1986   1992   1994   1996   1998   2002

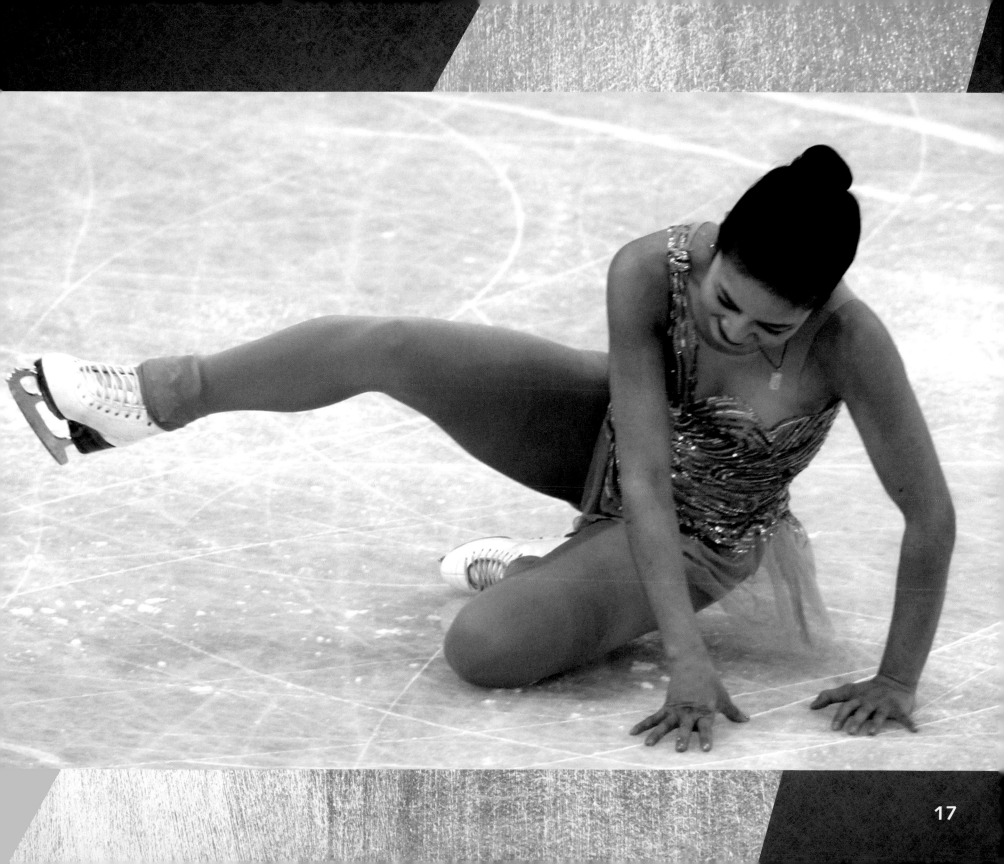

Life After Skating

Michelle took a break
from skating. She worked for
the U.S. government. She went
to college. She traveled
and talked about her life.

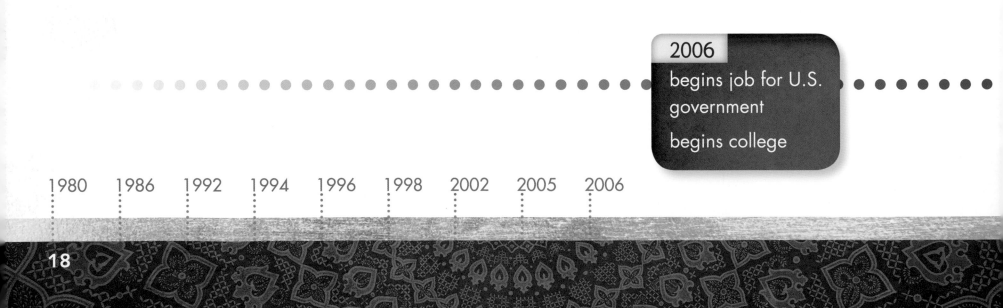

2006
begins job for U.S.
government

begins college

1980   1986   1992   1994   1996   1998   2002   2005   2006

Today Michelle works with people with disabilities. She helps them play sports. She is still known as one of the best figure skaters ever.

2011
joins board at Special Olympics

2017
entered into the California Sports Hall of Fame

1980   1986   1992   1994   1996   1998   2002   2005   2006

Michelle with athletes at a Special Olympics event

Glossary

bronze—kind of medal given to the third place finisher at the Olympics

disability—something that restricts people in what they can do, usually because of an illness, injury, or condition present at birth

gold—kind of medal given to the first place finisher at the Olympics

junior—person in a group with less experience

Olympics—a competition of many sports events held every four years in a different country; people from around the world compete against each other

senior—person in a group with more experience

silver—kind of medal given to the second place finisher at the Olympics

Read More

Schwartz, Heather E. *Singles Skating*. Figure Skating.
North Mankato, Minn.: Capstone, 2018.

Throp, Claire. *Figure Skating*. Winter Sports.
Chicago: Raintree, 2014.

Waxman, Laura Hamilton. *Figure Skating*. Winter Olympic Sports.
Mankato, Minn.: Amicus Ink, 2017.

Internet Sites

Use FactHound to find Internet Sites related to this book.

Visit *www.facthound.com*

Just type in 9781515799580 and go.

Check out projects, games and lots more at
www.capstonekids.com

Critical Thinking Questions

1. What if Michelle hadn't taken the senior test on her own? Do you think her life would have been different? Explain your answer.
2. Why do you think Michelle took a break from skating?
3. What does Michelle do today?

Index